CHOMP!
A Chewer's Guide to Gum

by Robert Young

illustrated by Hannah Mueller

Real Writing Unlimited
2014

For gum chewers everywhere.

With special thanks to Karen Antikajian, Ava Litton, Jennie Lower,
Rick Mann, Tom Reichert, Peggy Young, Tyler Young, and Kaiping Zhang.

Photos by Real Writing Press, the William Wrigley Jr., Company (p. 10),
Gary Duschl (p. 17), Chris Antes (l. p.32), Reuters (r. p. 32), and Jamie Marraccini (r. p. 33)

Text copyright © 2014 by Robert Young
Illustrations copyright © 2014 by Hannah Mueller

All rights reserved. No part of this publication may be reproduced in whole or in part, or stored in a retrieval system or transmitted in any form or by any means, electronically, mechanical, photocopying, recording, or otherwise without written permission from the copyright holder.

For permission contact Real Writing Press at areswhy@gmail.com

Presenting ... Gum!

Open the wrapper and the sweet smell tickles your nose. Pop a piece into your mouth and the zesty flavor explodes.
Chew, *chew*, CHOMP, CHOMP.
Ahh, the joy of chewing gum!

- ARABIC - AFRIKAANS - SWAHILI - FRENCH - HEBREW - TURKISH - GREEK -

SPANISH - CREOLE - ENGLISH - ICELANDIC - GAELIC - PORTUGUESE - MOROCCAN

You are not alone. People all around the world love gum. We chew more than a billion pounds of it a year. A billion! That's 50,000 tons of gum, the same weight as 40,000 school buses. Or, nearly 110,000 elephants!

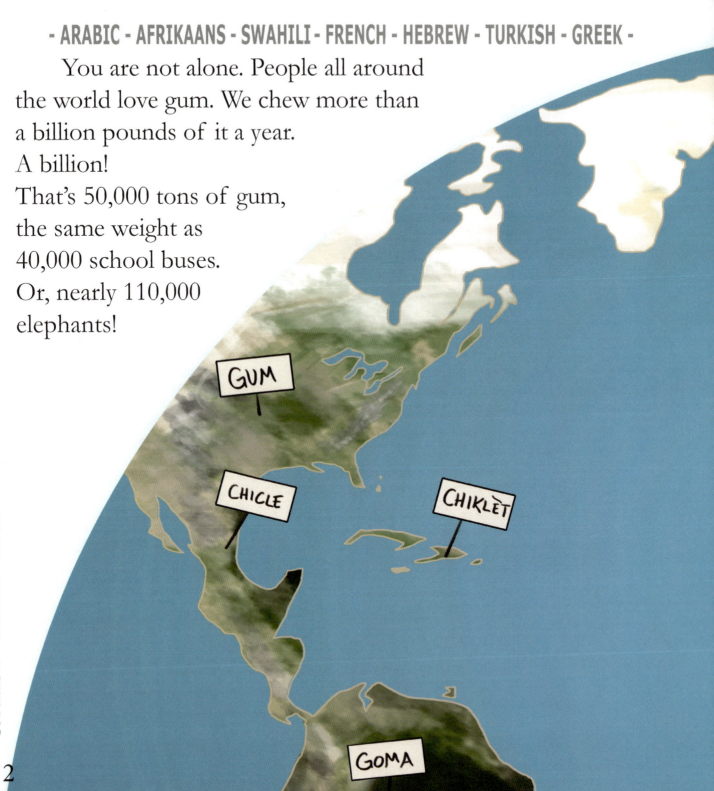

In the Beginning

It all starts with chewing. We all do it. Scientists say chewing is a natural urge. Chewing foods keeps us alive. But chewing also keeps our teeth clean and it helps us relax. Maybe this explains why, for thousands of years, humans have chewed nonfoods: sticks, leaves, animal gristle (chewy, inedible bits from meat), sweet grasses, and waxes. And then there was the resin, or sap, from trees.

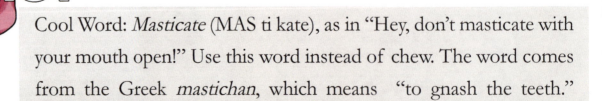

Cool Word: *Masticate* (MAS ti kate), as in "Hey, don't masticate with your mouth open!" Use this word instead of chew. The word comes from the Greek *mastichan*, which means "to gnash the teeth."

In North America, Native Americans chewed the sap of the spruce tree. The *Wampanoag* (wam pa NO ag) gave the Pilgrims their first taste of spruce gum in the early 1600s.

Chewing spruce gum grew as America did. In 1848, John Curtis and his son made the first spruce gum for sale in Bradford, Maine. Sales of State of Maine Pure Spruce Gum were good enough to hire more than 200 workers, invent gum-making machines, and build the world's first chewing gum factory.

But spruce gum did not last. The reason: newspapers. Spruce trees provided the paper for them. As newspapers became more popular, more trees were used so there weren't enough to get sap from. Luckily, this was not the end of gum forever.

Modern Gum

John Curtis also made gum from paraffin, a wax. He added sweet flavors, for the first time. But this gum needed the mouth's heat and moisture before it was ready to chew. Another material had to be found. And it was, thanks to a famous Mexican general.

Antonio Lopez de Santa Anna was well-known for his victory over the Texans at the Alamo in 1836. He had also served eleven terms as president of Mexico before being forced to leave the country.

FACT During Mexico's war against France in 1838, Santa Anna was hit by cannon fire. After doctors amputated his leg, Santa Anna had it buried with full military honors.

Santa Anna wanted to raise an army to take back Mexico. His plan: get money for his army by selling chicle for the U.S. to use instead of rubber.

In 1869, Santa Anna shared his plan with Thomas Adams, Sr., a New York inventor. Adams began working with the chicle, but he could not get it to do what rubber could. Santa Anna got tired of waiting and gave up.

But not Adams. One day he saw a girl buying paraffin gum in a drugstore. That reminded him that chicle had been chewed in Mexico for many years. Adams raced home and made his first batch of gum by heating chicle, rolling pieces into balls, and then wrapping them in tissue paper. Adams took his gum to the druggist and set a price: two for a penny. The gum was an instant success.

Gum Grows and Grows

New discoveries helped the gum business grow. Gum-makers added sugar and more flavors. After trying a sassafras (root beer) flavor, Thomas Adams made a licorice-flavored gum called Black Jack. In 1886, William White discovered a way to make flavors last longer by mixing them with corn syrup first.

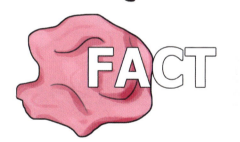

Black Jack was the first gum sold in packs of sticks. It is the oldest flavored gum still sold today.

Thomas Adams made the world-popular Yucatan, the first peppermint-flavored gum. William Wrigley, Jr. started selling Juicy Fruit and Wrigley's Spearmint in 1893. Franklin V. Canning invented Dentyne in 1899, and Henry Fleer made Chiclets, the first candy-coated gum.

Dentyne was the first "dental gum" because it had less sugar in it than other gum, which made it better for chewers' teeth.

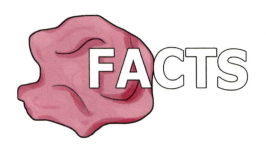

William Wrigley, Jr. was a great gum promoter. He offered free gifts—lamps, clocks, hatchets, slot machines—and took out ads in newspapers and on billboards. In Atlantic City, NJ Wrigley made a series of billboards that stretched one mile. In 1919, he sent free samples to every American listed in phone books.

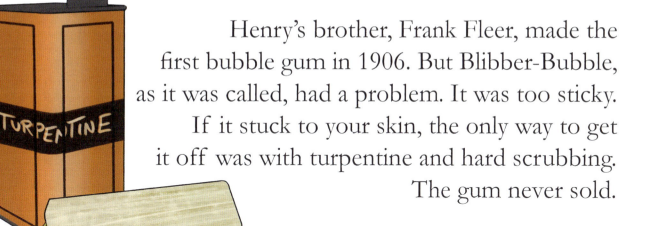

Henry's brother, Frank Fleer, made the first bubble gum in 1906. But Blibber-Bubble, as it was called, had a problem. It was too sticky. If it stuck to your skin, the only way to get it off was with turpentine and hard scrubbing. The gum never sold.

It took twenty-two years before a new, improved bubble gum was created.

Walter Diemer worked as an accountant at the Fleer Corporation, but he had a secret interest in making gum. After experimenting for more than a year, Diemer finally came up with a gum that was stretchy but not too sticky. Diemer did not think much about the color for his Double Bubble. He just grabbed the only color around — pink — and poured it into the batch.

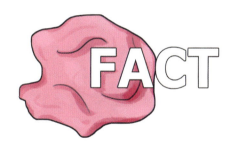

Double Bubble (and most other bubble gum) is still pink today.

Baseball pitchers Jim Bouton and Rob Nelson developed shredded gum in 1977. Their hope was to have this gum replace chewing tobacco used by some players.

More changes came along: sugarless gum in the 1950s, sour gum in the 1990s, more flavors, different colors, varied shapes. Gum-makers never stop working to change and improve gum. These changes will add to the long and sticky history of chewing gum.

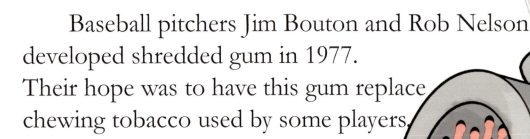

Great Moments in Gum History

1911 - British airmen use gum to patch up a hole in the dirigible (blimp) they are flying across the Atlantic. It saves their lives!

1921 - Heavyweight boxing champ Jack Dempsey chews gum to make his jaw muscles stronger. It works. George Carpetier breaks his thumb when he hits Dempsey in the jaw during their title fight. Dempsey knocks him out in the 4th round.

1929 - Double Bubble passes Tootsie Rolls as the world's most popular one-cent treat.

American explorer Admiral Richard Byrd takes gum to calm his nerves on his expedition to the south pole.

1930s - Gum companies start including picture cards — including baseball cards — with their bubble gum.

1931 - The Beech-Nut Company sponsors Amelia Earhart's cross-country flight on a autogiro.

1944 - Pennsylvania man loses teeth when his wad of bubble gum mysteriously explodes.

1953 - The Topps Company includes "Bazooka Joe" comics in its Bazooka bubble gum wrappers.

1958 - Lonnie Donegan records "Does Your Chewing Gum Lose Its Flavor (On the Bedpost Overnight)?" The song is a big hit in the UK and the US.

1965 - Gemini IV astronauts James McDivett and Ed White are the first to carry gum into space.

1974 - A pack of Wrigley's Juicy Fruit is the first product ever to be scanned. That pack now belongs to the Smithsonian's Museum of American History in Washington, DC.

Topps presents baseball star Willie Mays with the biggest chunk of bubble gum ever. It's made up of 10,000 pieces of Bazooka bubble gum.

1985 - Gum is used as evidence in an Oregon trial to help convict a man of murder.

1990 - Susan Montgomery Williams of Fresno, California is convicted of popping her gum too loud outside a courtroom.

1992 - Singapore, tired of the cost of clean-up, becomes the first country to ban gum.

1993 - Archeologists find the oldest piece of gum near Ellos, Sweden. The 9,000 year-old glob of sap had been sweetened with honey and chomped by a teenager.

1994 - Susan Montgomery Williams (see above) blows the world's biggest bubble (28 inches, 58.24 centimeters).

2000 - Joyce Samuels of Louisville, Kentucky blows the biggest nose bubble (11 inches, 27.94 centimeters).

2002 - A piece of bubble gum chewed by Luis Gonzalez of the Arizona Diamondbacks sells for $10,000 at a charity auction.

2004 - Singapore allows the sale of gum used for health reasons. Chad Fell blows the biggest hands-free bubble (20 inches, 50.8 centimeters).

2006 - Richard Walker wins the "Chomp Title" by chewing 135 sticks of bubble gum for eight hours.

2010 - Gary Duschl displays the world's longest gum wrapper chain in New York City. Made of 1,500,000 wrappers, the chain stretches 12 miles. Duschl spent more than 24,000 hours over 45 years to make the chain.

2012 - Bazooka Candy Brands replaces "Bazooka Joe" comics with brain teasers.

How Do They Do It?

Gum Guy here. There are many different kinds of gum, but they all have the same main ingredients: base (the chewy part of the gum), flavoring, softeners, and sweetener. Bubble gum has a stretchier base, making it easier to blow into bubbles.

Here's how it's made... Workers pour the pebble-like base into mixers, where it is heated as giant blades rotate. Sweeteners, softeners, and flavoring are added and mixed into a big doughy glob of gum.

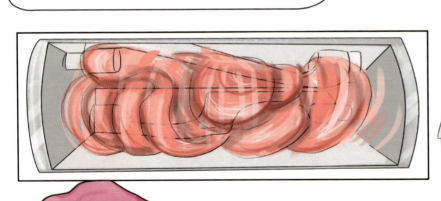

FACT

Until World War II, gum base came from tree saps. Since then, most gum base is made of plastics and rubbers.

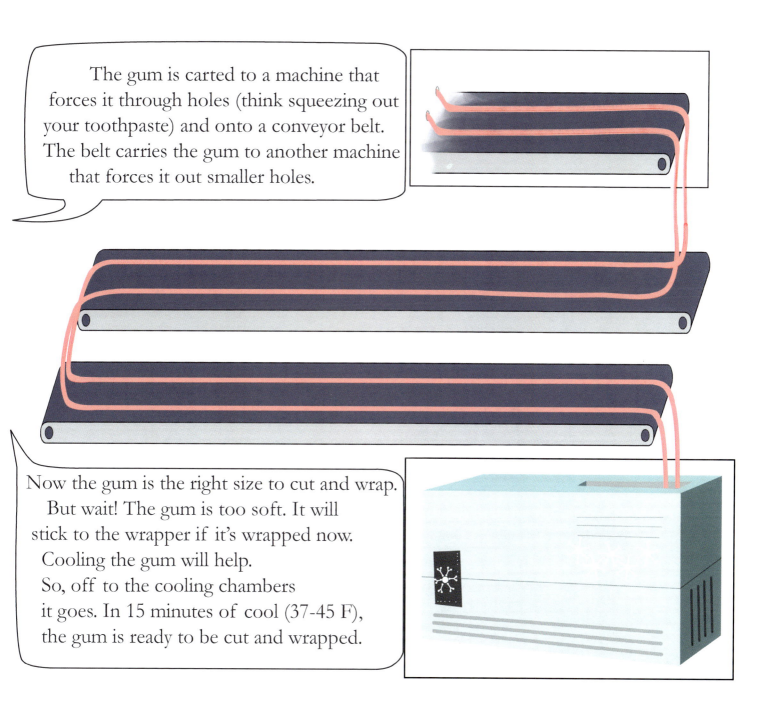

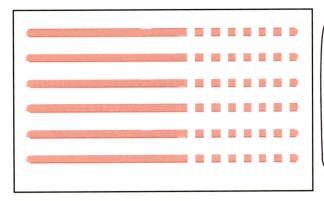

One machine can do both jobs. And fast, too! The machine cuts the gum, pushes each piece into a wax-paper wrapper, and then twists the end of the wrapper. All this happens in a fraction of a second.

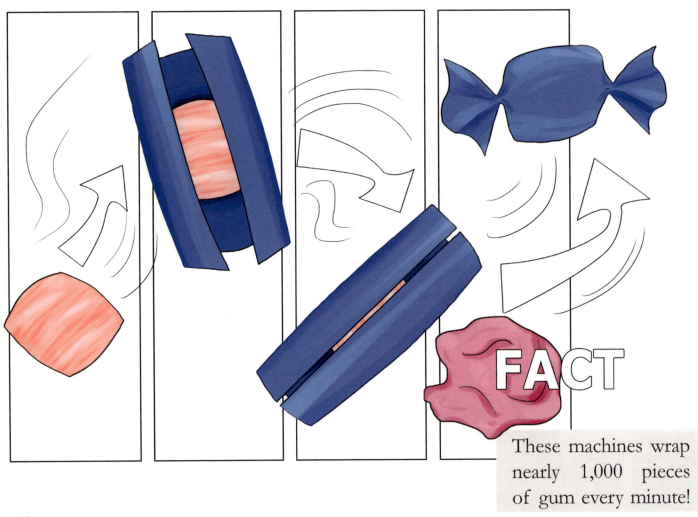

FACT

These machines wrap nearly 1,000 pieces of gum every minute!

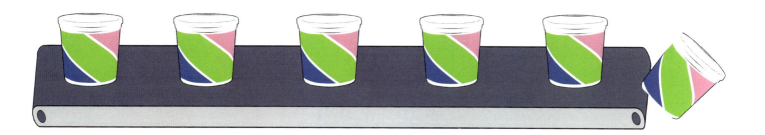

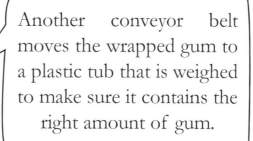
Another conveyor belt moves the wrapped gum to a plastic tub that is weighed to make sure it contains the right amount of gum.

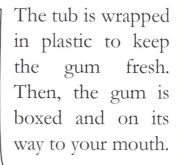
The tub is wrapped in plastic to keep the gum fresh. Then, the gum is boxed and on its way to your mouth.

To Chew or Not to Chew?

Think smart when it comes to chewing gum. Learn what doctors and dentists know. Find out what scientists are discovering in their research. Listen to your own body. Then decide.

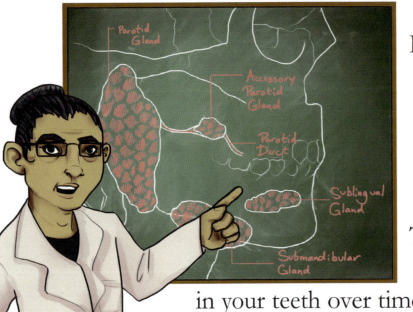

Dentists know that gum is pretty harmless, and that some gum helps your teeth. If gum has sugar, it mixes with bacteria in your mouth to make acid. This acid is strong enough to make holes (cavities) in your teeth over time. But chewing also causes your salivary glands to make three times more saliva, or spit. The saliva floods your mouth, washing away small pieces of food and making the acid weaker.

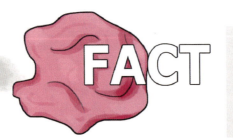

FACT: Salivary glands are small sacs in and around your mouth that make saliva. Each day your glands make enough saliva to fill a liter bottle.

Chewing sugarless gum is better. You get more saliva to wash away food, but you get it without the acid that creates cavities. Tests have shown that sugarless gum helps prevent cavities. Chewing it after meals when you can't brush your teeth is a good idea.

Some sugarless gums do even more. Gum made with xylitol, a non-sugar sweetener, helps prevent cavities by reducing bacteria. Gum made with Recaldent ™ helps protect you from cavities by making your teeth stronger.

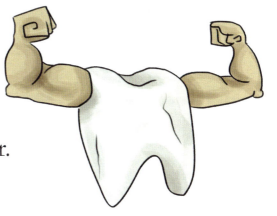

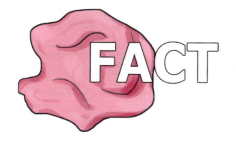

FACT How do you know what's in the gum you chew? It's easy. Just look at the list of ingredients on the pack. Sugar comes in many forms, including corn syrup, fructose, glucose, lactose, maltose, and sucrose.

Doctors know that chewing gum can be helpful to people who want to quit smoking or lose weight. But, there can be problems with gum, too. If you're allergic to the non-sugar sweeteners used in gum, you may get stomachaches or diarrhea.

Do you chew for long periods of time? If you do, you could get headaches or face pain.

Those pains are often caused by chewing on one side of your mouth. This makes facial muscles imbalanced, which can lead to pain.

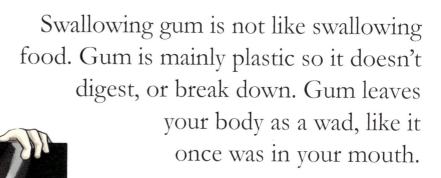

Swallowing gum is not like swallowing food. Gum is mainly plastic so it doesn't digest, or break down. Gum leaves your body as a wad, like it once was in your mouth.

Problems with swallowing gum are rare. One case involved a two-year-old girl who was rushed to the hospital with a painful, puffed-up stomach. Doctors found that something was blocking the girl's intestines. When the doctors removed the blockage, they found it was 100 g (3.5 oz) chunk of bubble gum. That's about twenty pieces!

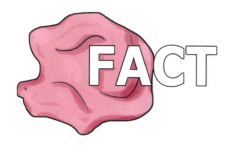

When is it safe for kids to start chewing gum? Some experts say at four years old. Others say six. Most agree that two-year-olds should not be chewing gum!

Scientists research gum and what happens when you chew.
Here's what their studies show:

> - CHEWING GUM CAN HELP YOU RELAX
>
> - CHEWING GUM CAN HELP YOU CONCENTRATE
>
> - CHEWING GUM CAN HELP YOU REMEMBER
>
> - CHEWING GUM CAN HELP YOU IMPROVE YOUR GRADES IN SCHOOL

Remember this: The word "can" is not the same as the word "will." You can't be certain that chewing gum will do all these things for you. But, you can do your own tests and see what the results are.

To chew or not to chew? That's up to you!

A Final Taste

HOW TO BLOW A BUBBLE:

- Put a piece of bubble gum in your mouth and start chomping.
- Chew for a couple of minutes until the gum is soft and moist.
- Move the gum to the front of your mouth. Use your front teeth to flatten the wad of gum.
- Using your tongue, push the gum against your front teeth. Flatten it some more with your tongue.
- Now, gently push your tongue into the gum (until it has a thin layer on it), open your mouth so that your tongue can come out, and blow.
- Voila! A bubble! Or not. If not, try again and again and again. It takes practice.

If you're having trouble making a bubble, check these things:
1. Your gum is soft and moist
2. Your gum is flat
3. Your tongue is covered by a thin layer of gum

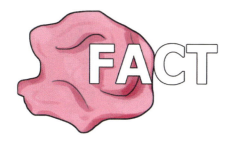

If the bubble (congratulations!) pops and sticks to your face (ick!), take the gum out of your mouth and dab it against the gum on your face. It will pick up the gum, just like magic!

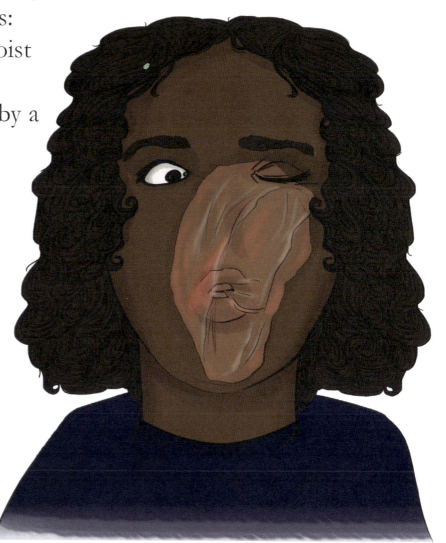

HOW TO HAVE YOUR OWN BUBBLE BLOWING CONTEST

What You Need:
- empty cereal box
- scissors
- paper clip or brad
- ruler or yardstick
- bubble gum
- and friends!

Now that you can blow bubbles, you can have your very own bubble blowing contest. You can do it during National Bubble Gum Week (the second week in March) or anytime.

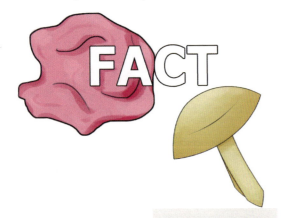

This is a brad   This is a paperclip

What You Do:

First, make the gum gauge to measure the bubbles. To make the gauge, cut open the cereal box so it lays flat. Then cut two one-inch wide strips the length of the box.

Line up the strips on top of each other. Paper clip the two together at one end (or use a brad for a more permanent gauge). Open the gauge by pulling each of the cardboard strips (jaws) in different directions.

Invite your friends to chew and blow bubbles. Taking turns, use the gauge to measure the bubbles. Open the gauge and carefully place the jaws on the outside of the widest part of the bubble. (Note: this can be tricky because the bubble can change sizes — or burst — very quickly.) Then, keeping the opening the same size, move the gauge to the ruler and measure the distance between the jaws (the diameter of the bubble). Biggest bubble wins!

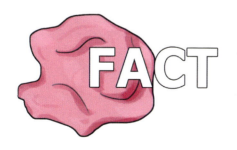

Are you a collector? Try collecting gum wrappers. Steve Fletcher, from London, holds the world record. He has 5,300 different wrappers from all over the world.

HOW TO CREATE GUM ART

Les Levine made it big in the 1970s. People around the world do it today. You, too, can create gum art!

Levine, a New York artist, made gum sculptures. He chewed pieces of gum, cast them in gold, mounted them, and displayed them in museums.

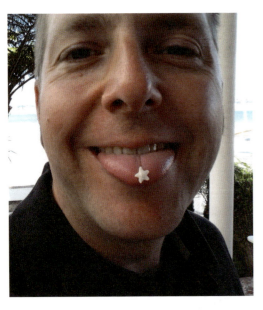

Artists all over the world use gum. Maurizio Savini (Italy) creates life-size gum sculptures while **Chris Antes** (U.S.) and Karoly Kiss (Romania) shape tiny figures in their mouths. Jason Kroenenwald (Canada) and **Anna Sofia Matveyeva** (Ukraine) use gum to make portraits of famous people.

Jamie Marraccini (U.S.) creates 3-D art, and Ben Wilson (U.K.) paints pieces of flattened gum on sidewalks.

People who visit **Gum Alley** in San Luis Obispo, California help create public gum art. Since the 1960s, thousands of pieces of gum have been "parked" on the brick walls that line this narrow alley. Beautiful! Other cities have walls of gum, too, including Greenville, Ohio and Seattle, Washington.

Here are two of the many ways to make your own gum art:

Way #1
What You Need: Poster board, gum of varied colors, clear acrylic spray, and a bowl of warm water.

What You Do:
　　Cut the poster board to the size you want your artwork. Chew, chew, chew the gum for at least 15 minutes until the flavor is gone. Dip the gum in the warm water to soften it then spread it onto the poster board in a shape that interests you. Keep chewing, dipping, and spreading until your masterpiece is complete.
To preserve your art, spray it with a couple coats of acrylic (follow directions on the can). Display it for all to see.

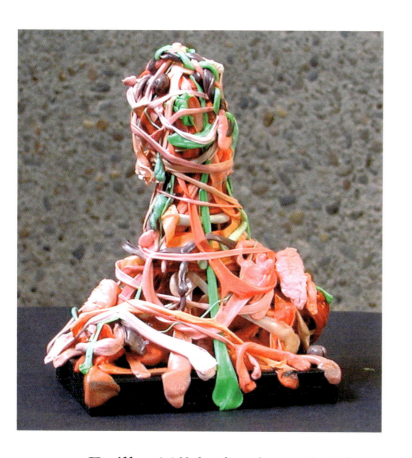

Way #2
What You Need:
A small block of wood (approx. 3"x5"), a 6" piece of ¼" dowel, wood glue, drill, spray paint (any color), clear acrylic spray, lots of gum, and a bowl of warm water.

What You Do:
Drill a ¼" hole about halfway through the center of the block. Glue the dowel stick into the hole. Let dry, then spray paint. This will be the stand for your GUM SCULPTURE. Now, start chewing the gum. Invite your friends and family to chew with you. When you're finished chewing, dip the gum into the water then "park it" on the stand, starting at the top of the dowel. Put the next piece on the first piece and so on until you have a beautiful sculpture made of chewing gum. When you have completed your work of art, spray it with the acrylic (follow directions on the can). Display proudly.

HOW TO REMOVE GUM FROM...

Clothes, fabrics, or carpet

Act fast! Pull off as much gum as you can before it dries. Then freeze the gum. You can do this by rubbing ice on it or putting the piece of clothing in the freezer until the gum hardens. Then, use a knife to gently scrape off the hardened gum. If there are small bits of gum left, use an old toothbrush to get them out.

Hair

No worries, scissors will NOT be used. Just some peanut butter. Rub a little bit (creamy preferred) on the gum and hair around it. Rub it well so the oil from the PB gets onto your hair. Then gently, very gently, pull the gum out. If the pb doesn't work, try a little bit of olive oil.

Pet Fur

See hair instructions

Wild Animals' Fur (bears, wolves, mountain lions)

Do not, repeat, DO NOT chew gum around these creatures!

HOW TO GET RID OF GUM

Yes, it's easy to just take gum out of your mouth and give it a toss or "park it" under the nearest seat. But, if you do this you're adding to the worldwide problem of gum garbage. That's right, millions of people around the globe get rid of their gum by sticking it or tossing it. Not good. You know that when you step on a sticky piece or touch a wad that was in someone else's mouth(yuck!). And what makes it worse: Gum takes hundreds of years to decompose, or break down.

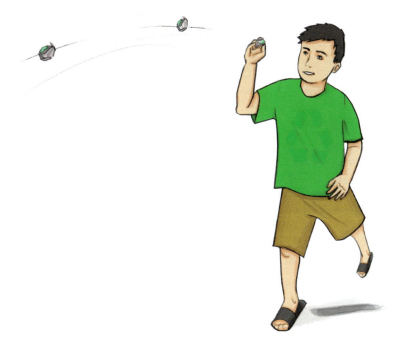

Companies around the world are working to solve the gum garbage problem. Some make biodegradable gum (that decomposes sooner). Others make containers or packages to put chewed gum into.

The simplest solution is to keep the wrapper to your gum. Then, when you are done chewing, just place the gum back in the wrapper and toss it in a garbage can. You have done your part to save the environment. The world thanks you!

Robert Young is the author of twenty-six books for kids. He wrote *Chomp! A Chewer's Guide to Gum* to celebrate the 25th anniversary of his his first work: *The Chewing Gum Book*. Robert makes his home in the Willamette Valley of Oregon. He loves traveling, swimming, chewing gum, and blowing bubbles.

Hannah Mueller was born in Trabuco Canyon, California and lives in Portland, Oregon. She studied digital art at the University of Oregon while working on *Chomp!* She rarely chews gum.

Resources

Books

Bubble Gum Science. Palo Alto, CA: Klutz, 1997.

Bubblemania by Lee Wardlaw. New York: Simon & Schuster, 1997.

The Chewing Gum Book by Robert Young. Minneapolis, MN: Dillon, 1989.

Chicle by Jennifer P. Matthews. Tucson, AZ: University of Arizona Press, 2009.

Pop! The Invention of Bubble Gum by Meghan McCarthy. New York: Simon & Schuster, 2010.

Websites

www.bubblegumheaven.com

www.chewinggumfacts.com

www.gleegum.com/make-your-own-gum-kit.htm

www.gumart.com

www.gumassociation.org

www.gumwrapper.com

Made in the USA
Columbia, SC
17 January 2018